CITY GEESE

CITY GEESE

by Ron Hirschi • Color photographs by Galen Burrell

Dodd, Mead & Company • New York

For Brian and Leanne

Text copyright © 1987 by Ron Hirschi
Photographs copyright © 1987 by Galen Burrell
All rights reserved
No part of this book may be reproduced in any form
without permission in writing from the publisher
Distributed in Canada by
McClelland and Stewart Limited, Toronto
Printed in Hong Kong by South China Printing Company
Designed by Charlotte Staub

1   2   3   4   5   6   7   8   9   10

Library of Congress Cataloging-in-Publication Data

Hirschi, Ron.
  City geese.

  Includes index.
  Summary: Follows a flock of Canada geese through a year in an
urban environment, from nesting and molting to feeding flights
and the formation of new pairs in winter.
  1. Canada goose—Juvenile literature.   2. Urban fauna—
Colorado—Fort Collins—Juvenile literature. 3. Birds—Colorado
—Fort Collins—Juvenile literature. [1. Canada goose.   2. Geese]
I. Burrell, Galen, ill.   II. Title.
QL696.A52H57 1987   598.4'1   86-19676
ISBN 0-396-08819-8

CONTENTS

PROLOGUE

The beauty and haunting call of the Canada goose have long been symbols of distant, northern wilderness. We have changed these wild places forever because of our changes to the land.

But, there is no need to change the wilderness symbol; Canada geese thrive even though we have destroyed breeding grounds and once hunted them without concern for their future.

Now, the honking of Canada geese awakens people in the hearts of cities such as Fort Collins, Colorado, where this story is set. Here, and in many North American and European cities, their presence has created a wilderness in our midst and their morning calls are as welcome and uplifting as their graceful flight.

Goose flock returning to snow-covered grass surrounding the city pond at Fort Collins, Colorado.

MORNING CALL

Above: The flock begins to wake up.
Left: Frost paints crystal designs on a Canada goose.

Although spring is about to begin, a thin layer of fresh snow covers the ground. On the shores of the city pond, frost paints its crystal designs on the feathers of a Canada goose.

The goose spent the night with its head and legs tucked close to its body. A layer of soft feathers insulates the goose from the cold. Gray, chocolate brown, and white outer feathers cover this fluffy down, shielding the bird from the icy breeze like a Windbreaker. Goose feathers are also excellent raincoats; they shed water and protect inner feathers from the morning frost.

As the sun rises and frost begins to melt, a few geese raise their heads. The flock begins to wake up.

One bird, then another, stretches and flaps its broad wings. They look this way, then that, inspecting their surroundings for possible danger.

As more geese wake up, small groups of

9

The geese are anxious to leave...

...and flap their wings in preparation for flight.

A pair leaps into the wind.

birds stand and stretch. They rustle their feathers, then waddle to the water's edge. It is a cold morning for a bath. But the near-freezing water drips off their backs as the geese dip headfirst into the chilly pond, then flap their wings while standing in the shallows.

Soon the entire flock is awake.

The pond stirs like a giant soup bowl as all the geese wade through the shallows, then swim into deeper water. Their broad feet are strong paddles.

Anxious to leave for the distant fields for breakfast, the geese begin to squabble among themselves. But single birds won't fly until others are ready. So the birds wait, watching one another in anticipation, as each goose adjusts its feathers for flight.

Suddenly, a pair of geese leaps into the wind, scooping and splashing the water with each kicking foot. With wing tips stretched out and forward, the birds pull their bodies into the air and lift off, honking a loud call to the flock below. Other birds join them and soon, small flocks of three, ten, and more fill the air until all the birds have left the pond.

The geese fly above the pond and gather into a single flock as they circle the city on their strong, broad wings. When they turn to fly to the farm fields at the edge of town, their morning call can be heard in backyards, along busy streets, at the schoolyard, and in the city playground.

Ka-ronk! Ka-ronk! Ka-ronk! High overhead, the morning call of the city goose signals the beginning of a new day.

As the call fades in the distance, the beauty of their line of flight is a strong memory. But the flock will return. By evening, they fly back to the city pond. There the geese will raise their young, spend the summer, and endure the frosty mornings of city winters in the months and years ahead.

Flocks fly to and from the city.

NESTING SEASON

Above: Goose on a ground nest.
Left: Winter flocks.

Like crowds of commuters, goose flocks fly to and from the city. Throughout the last days of winter, the chorus of honking calls can be heard above traffic noise on streets below, and calls of individual birds seem inseparable from the sound of the flock.

The geese seem inseparable from one another too.

Each large flock is actually many flocks in one. Family members fly together in these small flocks, and each bird knows its relatives well. They fly as one, but this family unity gradually breaks down as spring mornings brighten earlier and earlier. Eventually, the sound of individual birds can be heard more clearly, as pairs break away from the flock and the nesting season begins.

Geese usually mate for the first time when they are three years old. But younger birds sometimes play at nest building. They pick up dry grass and toss it over their shoulders

15

A gander threatens.

toward pretend nest sites. Then they tuck the loose pieces around their bodies, creating "make-believe" nests. These first nests may never hold eggs, but they do help young geese learn valuable skills needed to become successful parents in the future.

More importantly, the young goose gets to know its surroundings as it goes through the steps in nest construction. Searching for nest material at the edge of the pond, it learns where food and danger are located in relation to a likely place to nest. Even if she doesn't raise a brood this year, the young female is likely to return to this same place next spring to build a real nest with a mate she has chosen from the flock.

Older birds may have learned nesting skills in past years, and often reuse the same nesting place, but they still have difficulties. They often must fight, sometimes even to the death, for their right to these nesting places.

After defending their nest, the pair returns together.

Fights for nesting places seem to go on forever early in the nesting season, especially near the highly valued nest boxes built for the geese by people. Wings flap, hissing threats are answered with battle, and some aggressive birds chase their rivals, then grasp them by the neck with a bill that is strong enough to inflict considerable injury.

In the midst of these battles for nests there are calmer moments.

A successful pair of geese goes together to the nest box they defended so viciously. The pair then calls to one another, singing a duet of deep-throated honks and soft yips that rise gently from the shores of the city pond. This peaceful duet is thought to further strengthen the bond between male and female, a bond that keeps the pair together for life.

The male stands guard near the nest during the month the female sits on her eggs. He honks loudly if she gets up to leave and may try to lead her back to the nest. But she remains persistent, covers her eggs with a soft layer of down, and the pair swims off together.

After feeding on tender, spring plants in the shallows, the pair returns to the nest. Only the female cares for the eggs and she stands over them after each feeding trip, gently removing the blanket of down. Water drips from her breast feathers, adding a thin layer of dampness thought to help the eggs hatch.

Returning to her nest, the goose lifts the down blanketing the eggs and settles to begin incubation. She also turns the eggs, rolling them with her feet or gently poking them with her bill to make sure the eggs are warm all over.

Gander displays his cheek patches like an elk its antlers.

All the while, the male waits.

Should danger approach, he threatens with neck outstretched, head low, and feathers ruffled in a way that makes him look twice his size. A display of his clean, white cheek patches is thought to be respected by other geese just as the horns and antlers of bighorn sheep and elk are respected threat symbols to their rivals. To animals other than geese, the power of the goose wing is also respected.

Protective and effective fathers, ganders, as males are called, have been known to defend their nests in remote areas from skunks, coyotes, and bald eagles. City ganders are just as devoted to their nesting mate and offspring and protect her and the eggs from unleashed dogs, raccoons, or people who come too close.

Safe within their protective shells, young geese begin their peeping calls two or three days before they hatch. With little room or

20

Gosling is joined by brothers and sisters that hatch a few hours later.

strength, they start pecking at the inside of the shells, spending as long as a day and a half chipping their way to freedom.

Nest mates hatch within a few hours of one another. Emerging from the isolation of their shells, the nestlings immediately start to get to know one another and their parents by sight and by sound.

Goslings swim with no coaching at all.

Left: A goose family walks to the city pond.

Goslings stay in the nest for their first day, but curiosity soon leads them into the pond. With no experience or coaching from their parents, the young birds can feed, drink, and swim on their own. Parents may pull up plants for them, but the goslings are quick to feed by tipping up their tails and reaching beneath the surface to pluck water plants with their own tiny bills.

At night and in the rain, the mother goose shields her downy young from the cold. They lack the protective layer of outer feathers, so she tucks the yellow goslings beneath her wings. Peering out at the world from the safety of their mother's feathers, the young geese listen and watch as spring days grow warmer.

The chorus of frogs, hum of dragonfly wings, and the distant street noises all mingle to become the goslings' familiar evening sounds.

Within their first few weeks, the goslings'

Goslings on a city pond.

yellow down fades to gray. After three weeks, blackish tail feathers appear. Breast feathers grow out at about four weeks and by the sixth week, the distinctive white cheek patches of an adult goose can be seen on the young birds.

By early summer the young geese are barely recognizable from their parents to people who come to watch and to feed the birds at the city pond. But, the geese know one another well by now.

They call softly, *Kum! Kum! Kum!*, to attract a family member. Then, the family flock swims together as it would on a wilderness lake far to the north, on a prairie marsh, or on a gentle stream within the boundaries of a national park. For reasons no one can explain, the geese form the same strong bond with their places of birth as they do with their family members. Because the city is their home, these geese will remain here for many nesting seasons to come.

By early summer young geese are barely recognizable from their parents.

SUMMER
DAYS

Above: Where have the city geese gone?
Left: Flight.

Flight. Nothing, not even its distinctive call, seems as important to the goose as flight. Yet, during much of the calm warmth of summer, geese cannot fly.

No honking flocks circle the city. No ganders fly to search for their mates. No V-shaped formations pass overhead as morning commuters drive into the city to begin their day. It is as if the beauty of geese in flight has vanished from the city's skyline forever.

Where have the city geese gone?

Some of the birds that did not nest have flown to lakes or reservoirs outside the city. But the nesting birds remain. Adults cannot fly now because they lose their flight feathers soon after the young ones leave the nest. As if experiencing life as a gosling one more time, the parent geese remain in this flightless, and somewhat helpless condition, until their feathers grow back in about five to six weeks.

27

A gentle breeze lifts a loose feather during the molting season.

As the adult birds gradually lose and grow new feathers during this molting period, gentle breezes lift the loose feathers. You might find the long, dark, wing feathers of a flightless goose along the shore, or those of mute swans or mallard ducks that also nest within the city.

You might also find the adult birds and their goslings swimming quietly on city pond.

Their silence may help parent birds avoid calling attention to their young and the dangers of predators. They also may not call because they cannot fly.

As the goslings grow and their own coats of feathers rapidly change, most of them remain under the watchful eye of their parents. Close ties between adults and young grow stronger and goslings continue to get to know one another. But for some geese, getting to know *new* brothers and sisters must be a difficult task. This is especially true within goose families that double or even triple in size from one summer day to the next through adoption.

Goose adoption is common and the largest families might grow to include as many as twenty or more goslings.

How do parents care for so many young geese and where do the new family members come from?

Like the best teacher on a day care field trip, some adult geese seem especially able to keep young ones together. Maybe these superparents come from large families. No one knows. We do know that goslings become attached to new parents in several ways.

Especially mean ganders will sometimes take goslings away from inexperienced, less aggressive parents. Adoption also takes place when young adult birds seem to give up their offspring without a struggle. Still other goslings are tended by geese with no offspring of their own.

Adopted groups may number twenty or more young geese.

29

By the time summer is at its peak, city goose families are grouped in as many ways as the humans visiting the city pond. Yearling geese gather like teen-agers; old geese that have lost their mates stand alone; young pairs swim with their three to five goslings safely guarded; and large family flocks might include parents with their own young ones and many adopted goslings.

Soon, the single birds and goose families gather in larger flocks. Yearlings often rejoin their parents at this time as the long summer silence and flightlessness come to an end.

Older geese preen their new set of flight feathers, flap, and stretch. The young birds stretch too. All are ready for their first flight together to nearby areas.

The gathering birds stir the surface of the city pond once again and they toss their heads, waving their bills from side to side as a signal of their intention to fly. Then, they spring to the air, calling to one another in

A single goose.

30

Parents and young on first flight of late summer.

a familiar voice that signals the approach of autumn. Climbing skyward, the flock's honking calls are heard once again above the sounds of the city.

KEEP OFF GRASS

AUTUMN FLIGHTS

Above: Some people disapprove of geese on grass.

Left: City geese flying to farm fields at the edge of town.

L ight rain falls, gathering in puddles along the walk to the city pond. You might leap over each pool of water, flying for one, brief moment.

High overhead, the goose flock flies over the city, soaring past on their own autumn flights.

The geese travel in larger groups now. Several families fly together to nearby lakes, rivers, or to the farm fields on the edge of town. Looking down from above, each wet place must look as tiny as a puddle from their height. But the geese know which is big enough for a landing. They also seem to know where they are welcome.

Long before the city grew large enough to need schools, golf courses, or parks, the geese could land freely on any field. Then they chose places that gave them a clear view in all directions so they might see any approaching predators.

Now they face new dangers.

Geese in corn field.

Within the city limits, some people disapprove of goose droppings left behind by the flocks. Some golfers, park managers, and landscapers chase the geese away from their favorite green grass.

Outside the city limits, the goose flocks descend on farm fields to feed, especially those with geese already standing among the corn stubble. Birds flying in will choose these fields first because they are attracted by the geese on the ground. They also return to familiar fields.

Circling from high above the corn fields,

Single geese circle back to be with their fallen partners.

Loss of a mate.

the geese set their wings to land. Their powerful wing beats stop. The trailing edges of their wing feathers arch forward. The broad cups that are formed brake their forward motion. Then, the birds drop to the ground in hopes of finding a meal.

Sometimes, they only find hunters waiting and the birds are greeted by shotgun blasts that flare from within a circle of plastic goose decoys meant to trick the flock into a landing.

Should one goose crumple, fallen by the hunter's gun, its mate will circle back. Drawn by its need to stay with its lifelong companion, the single goose seems to ignore the sound of shooting and often returns to its own death.

Geese occasionally die when they fly into buildings or wires on foggy nights. They are also killed by dogs or hit by cars. But, hunting remains the major cause of death, even for the city flocks that live where larger and

In the gray stillness of January, a winter pair walks together.

Left: Autumn flock.

larger tracts of land are being closed to hunting as homes and businesses spread across former farm fields.

City goose flocks were originally introduced to these developing areas for hunters to shoot. Now, the flocks remaining in parks, golf courses, and other patches of open land live within a new kind of wildlife refuge.

These urban wildlife sanctuaries lack boundaries, entry fees, and campgrounds, but they are as important to geese as any national park and have helped Canada goose numbers increase.

Geese must continually search for new refuges as the city grows, eliminating their feeding grounds. Autumn feeding flights to the edge of the city must take new directions each year and for birds that have lost their mates, these new flights may be made in solitude. Still, the single goose that survives will take refuge in the flock and may seek a new companion in the winter months ahead.

WINTER VISITORS

Above: Wigeon pair. Wigeon are common companions of winter geese.

Left: Mallards landing in flock of geese.

Wheee Whee Wheow!
Wheee Whee Wheow!!
Wheee Whee Wheow!!!

The whistling call of wigeons mingles with the sun that just now pierces the morning fog. Flying from their northern breeding grounds, these ducks gather with the city goose flocks. Grazing alongside the much larger goose, the wigeon calmly plucks the sparse winter grass with its pale, blue-gray bill.

Nearby, mallards, drakes with their purple-green heads glistening, land in the midst of a more wary flock of geese from far to the north. The mallards seem to be less at home with the larger birds. The wild goose flock also seems less at home in city park than the geese grazing with the wigeons.

These northern geese swim quickly, staring nervously at each new sound. Suddenly they fly and the mallard slumps to the water to avoid being kicked on the top of its head.

Geese and wigeons feed at the city playfield.

Like thousands of other northern geese, the wild flock once bypassed the city on its way to traditional wintering grounds farther south. Little by little, they have become less frightened by people, traffic, and barking dogs, and they stop more frequently, attracted by the sight and sound of the city geese.

Hunters to the south may complain, but

goose numbers now increase as winter flocks gather in the safety of the city. Despite the snow and cold, these wild geese remain, some gathering only in the most remote patches of land at the edge of town. Others, however, mix freely with the tamest flock of city geese.

The mixed flocks huddle together as snow blankets the hillside surrounding the city pond. They await warmer days when most of the northern birds will migrate.

But, some of the winter visitors will stay behind since this is the season for new pairs to form.

In the gray stillness of January, the winter pairs walk together. No one knows how they choose one another or why some pairs decide to stay here in the city rather than to fly to Montana, Wyoming, or Canada. We only know that city life seems to be the way of life for more and more of these wild and beautiful birds.

Some geese gather in remote patches of land at the edge of town.

EPILOGUE: GOOSE CITY

L ong ago, Aleutian Islanders tended small flocks of Canada geese just as many people now keep domestic geese for food or feathers. But, the Aleut way of life was forever changed by Russian and American settlers and traders. So, too, was the life of the geese that inhabited the Aleutian Islands; today, the distinctive subspecies of that area is rare and endangered.

Other people also herded flocks of Canada geese, fattening them for markets in Canada and the United States shortly before the turn of the century. The birds were easily tamed and bred in captivity and descendants of those captive flocks may be among the geese which now fly freely in city parks.

Because there was such great demand for geese, many people also hunted wild flocks for market, competing with the poultry farmers. In 1895 nearly fifty thousand geese were sold at markets in San Francisco and Los Angeles alone. Such a tremendous demand soon placed goose populations in a perilous position. Fortunately, hunting was regulated and the Canada goose did not become extinct.

Still, nesting populations in the United States were severely threatened and did not begin to recover until reintroductions began in the 1940s and 1950s, especially near urban areas. Today, some people complain because geese seem to be "too plentiful." But, they are still far less abundant than in the past. Also, there are many places where geese have not returned and where you might urge them to be reintroduced.

Cities where geese live usually consider the goose as a visitor. But, to the birds, many towns that offer goose nest boxes and plenty of open space must seem to be goose cities. As long as we welcome their presence, the morning call and the graceful line of flight of the city goose will soar forever.

GLOSSARY

Aleutian Islands.   The Aleutians string westward from the southwestern tip of Alaska to the edge of Asia. This is the nesting home of the Aleutian Canada goose.

Down.   The soft, underfeathers of birds that are especially thick on waterbirds, such as ducks and geese.

Gander.   Male goose; female is called goose.

Gosling.   Young goose.

Grazing.   Feeding on grass and other low-growing plants.

Molting.   Process of growing new feathers.

Species.   A single kind of plant or animal.

Subspecies.   All animals vary. Some, like the Canada goose, vary a great deal. Birds nesting in the Aleutian Islands weigh about four or five pounds and have distinctive white collars at the bases of their black necks. Geese in other places may weigh as much as twenty pounds. Each different group of birds, such as the distinctive birds of the Aleutians, are known as subspecies. Many scientists agree that there are eight subspecies; all are part of the single species, Canada goose.

INDEX

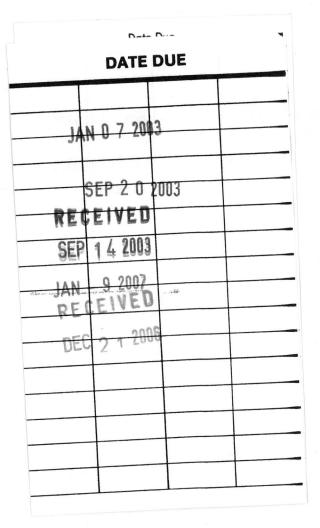

Date Due

DATE DUE

JAN 0 7 2003			
SEP 2 0 2003			
RECEIVED			
SEP 1 4 2003			
JAN 9 2007			
RECEIVED			
DEC 2 1 2006			